ANCIENT AND MEDIEVAL PEOPLE

The Medieval Knights

Louise Park
and Timothy Love

Marshall Cavendish
Benchmark
New York

This edition first published in 2010 in the United States of America by Marshall Cavendish Benchmark.

Marshall Cavendish Benchmark
99 White Plains Road
Tarrytown, NY 10591
www.marshallcavendish.us

All Internet sites were available and accurate when sent to press.

First published in 2009 by
MACMILLAN EDUCATION AUSTRALIA PTY LTD
15–19 Claremont Street, South Yarra 3141

Visit our website at www.macmillan.com.au or go directly to www.macmillanlibrary.com.au

Associated companies and representatives throughout the world.

Library of Congress Cataloging-in-Publication Data

Park, Louise, 1961–
    The medieval knights / by Louise Park and Timothy Love.
        p. cm. – (Ancient and medieval people)
    Includes index.
    ISBN 978-0-7614-4444-2
    1. Knights and knighthood–Juvenile literature. 2. Civilization,
Medieval–Juvenile literature. I. Love, Timothy. II. Title.
    CR4513.P36 2009
    909.07–dc22
                        2008055777

Edited by Julia Carlomagno
Text and cover design by Cristina Neri, Canary Graphic Design
Page layout by Cristina Neri, Canary Graphic Design
Photo research by Legend Images
Illustrations by Colby Heppéll, Giovanni Caselli, and Paul Konye

Printed in the United States

Acknowledgments
The author and the publisher are grateful to the following for permission to reproduce copyright material:

Front cover photo: Bodiam Castle © Jeremy Edwards/iStockphoto; parchment © Selahattin BAYRAM/ iStockphoto

Photos courtesy of: Background photos throughout: old paper © peter zelei/iStockphoto; mosaic tiles © Hedda Gjerpen/iStockphoto; dagger © Mark Hilverda/iStockphoto; knights on horseback silhouette © A-Digit/iStockphoto; knights and castle silhouette © bubaone/iStockphoto; sword © Brendon De Suza/iStockphoto; Coo-ee Historical Picture Library, **12**, **14**, **16**, **18**, **19**, **20**, **22**, **23**, **24**, **25**, **26**, **28**, **29**; French School/Getty Images, **30**; French School/Getty Images; Giovanni Caselli's Universal Library Unlimited, **17**, **21**; Hulton Archive/Getty Images via iStockphoto, **6**; © Jeremy Edwards/iStockphoto, **4** (castle); © Alan McCredie/iStockphoto, **15**; © Roberto A Sanchez/iStockphoto, **7**; Photolibrary © North Wind Picture Archives/Alamy, **8**, **11**; Photolibrary/Mary Evans Picture Library, **9**, **10**, **13**.

Sources for quotes used in text: The knights's code of chivalry adapted from www.middle-ages.org.uk/ knights-code-of-chivalry.htmcsadas, **11**.

While every care has been taken to trace and acknowledge copyright, the publisher tenders their apologies for any accidental infringement where copyright has proved untraceable. Where the attempt has been unsuccessful, the publisher welcomes information that would redress the situation.

The authors and publisher wish to advise that to the best of their ability they have tried to verify dates, facts, and the spelling of personal names and terminology. The accuracy and reliability of some information on ancient civilizations is difficult in instances where detailed records were not kept or did not survive.

1 3 5 6 4 2

Contents

Glossary Words

When a word is printed in **bold**, you can look up its meaning in the Glossary on page 31.

Who Were the Medieval Knights?

The medieval knights were powerful **warriors** who fought on behalf of their king and their country. They fought on horseback to defend the king's **territory** and castles.

King Charlemagne's Kingdom

Medieval knights were established by King Charlemagne. Charlemagne's kingdom extended across much of western Europe, including France and parts of Italy and Germany. Medieval knights came from the countries that formed part of Charlemagne's kingdom and for hundreds of years they were influential across Europe. They also fought in **military campaigns** in the Middle East.

WHAT'S IN A NAME?
Medieval Knight
The word *medieval* comes from the Latin words **Medium Aevum**, which means "middle ages." The word *knight* comes from the Old English word *cniht*. It means "pageboy" or "servant."

Medieval Knights Timeline

774
Charlemagne uses mounted warriors in battle

1000s
A new order of armored knights appears in Europe. The first **tournaments** are held to train knights for battle.

1118
The Knights Templar, a military **religious order**, is formed to fight in the Crusades

750 CE — 1000 — 1100 — 1200

1066
The Normans invade England and win the Battle of Hastings

1095
Medieval knights fight in the Crusades

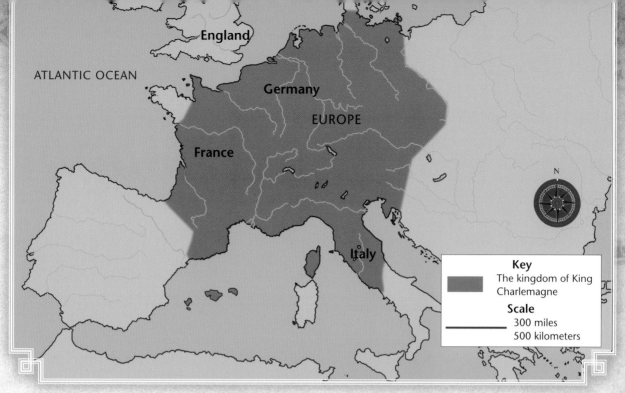

Medieval knights were found in many European countries, where they defended the lands within King Charlemagne's kingdom.

Knights in Medieval Times

Around 774 CE, King Charlemagne started using **mounted** warriors in battle. These warriors became known as knights. Knights, or armored warriors who fought on horseback, emerged during the 1000s, or the medieval times. These knights fought until the 1500s, when they were replaced with professional soldiers in armies.

In the beginning, any wealthy man could become a knight. The king would also reward his bravest and most loyal soldiers by making them into knights. Sometimes knights themselves would make other men into knights. Eventually, knights were chosen only from the families of other knights. These families became known as the **nobility**. If a man was born into the nobility, then he became a knight.

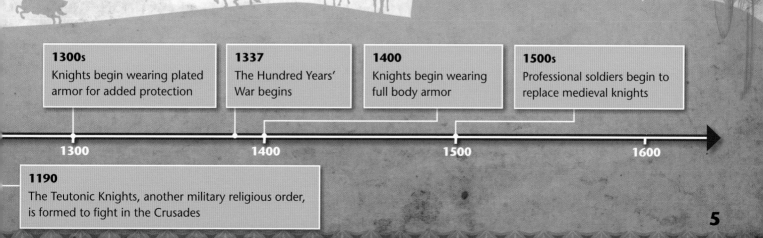

1300s
Knights begin wearing plated armor for added protection

1337
The Hundred Years' War begins

1400
Knights begin wearing full body armor

1500s
Professional soldiers begin to replace medieval knights

1300   1400   1500   1600

1190
The Teutonic Knights, another military religious order, is formed to fight in the Crusades

IN PROFILE: King Charlemagne

In Profile

NAME: King Charlemagne
ALSO KNOWN AS: Charles the Great
BORN: Between 742 and 747
DIED: 814

K ing Charlemagne began the era of the medieval knights. He is remembered for extending his kingdom through successful military campaigns and introducing many new ideas.

During his **reign** King Charlemagne gained and **consolidated** more territory than any other king or queen of his time. His fierce military leadership and his reputation as a fair and just king earned him the respect of the nobility and the awe of both enemies and **allies**.

Notable Moment

King Charlemagne consolidated a large portion of Europe and ruled over many groups of people. His titles included:

❖ King of the Franks (people in western Europe and parts of central Europe)

❖ King of the Lombards (people in lower Germany and northern Italy)

❖ First Emperor of the Holy Roman Empire (people in parts of central Europe)

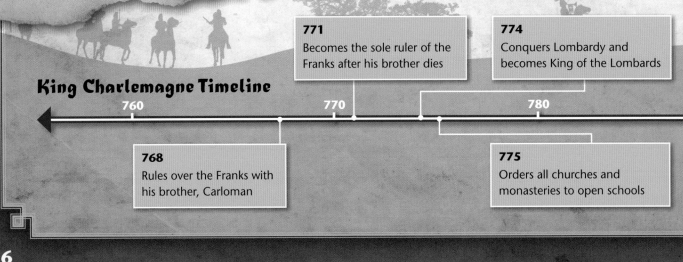

King Charlemagne Timeline

771
Becomes the sole ruler of the Franks after his brother dies

774
Conquers Lombardy and becomes King of the Lombards

760　　　　770　　　　780

768
Rules over the Franks with his brother, Carloman

775
Orders all churches and monasteries to open schools

Introducing New Ideas

Charlemagne introduced many new ideas during his reign. These included:

❖ promoting the arts

❖ encouraging the teaching of reading and writing

❖ setting up the first monastic schools, which taught religion to children

❖ preserving many Latin documents

❖ creating a new system of money, which included pounds, shillings, and pence

The system of money introduced by Charlemagne was used in Britain until 1971, when it was replaced with another system called the decimal system.

Statues of Charlemagne are found across Europe, including this one in St. Peter's Basilica in Rome.

What You Should Know About...

Charlemagne and His Warriors

❖ Charlemagne rewarded his mounted warriors by giving them land. In return, the warriors had to fight whenever they were needed. They also had to remain loyal to Charlemagne. This arrangement continued throughout most of the Middle Ages.

❖ The warriors fought eighteen battles against the **Saxons**. It is believed that during one battle, Charlemagne ordered the killing of approximately 4,500 Saxon prisoners in one day.

800	810	820

791–796
Launches successful military campaigns against Austria and Hungary

800
Crowned Emperor of the Holy Roman Empire by Pope Leo II

814
Dies and leaves power to his only son, Louis

Becoming a Knight

Boys who were to become knights served an **apprenticeship** in another knight's castle. During their apprenticeship, they learned the basic skills needed to become a knight.

From Page to Squire

A boy became a page at the age of seven and served in this role for seven years. A page learned:

❖ how to behave and practice good manners

❖ how to ride a horse while carrying a **lance**

❖ how to fight, practicing with wooden swords and shields

At the age of fourteen, a successful page became known as a squire. A squire was expected to:

❖ serve his master loyally

❖ help his master prepare for battle

❖ look after his master's armor and horses

❖ behave respectfully to ladies

In return, a knight taught a squire what he needed to know to become a knight. Knights practiced fighting, wrestling, **jousting**, and sword skills with their squires.

This knight is shown with his page on the right and his squire on the left.

WHAT'S IN A NAME?

Squire

The word *squire* comes from the French word **ecuyer**. It means "shield-bearer."

From Squire to Knight

Squires were made into knights when they turned twenty-one, or when they had acquired the necessary skills. Squires became knights in an event called a dubbing ceremony. During this ceremony, a knight or the king would tap the squire on the shoulder with a sword. The newly dubbed knight was then presented with riding spurs and a sword. Often, a celebration took place afterward and the new knight demonstrated his skills. Once a squire was knighted, he was called "Sir."

Knights were expected to teach their squires about a knight's duties and responsibilities.

Quick Facts

Were Squires Always Knighted in a Ceremony?

Many squires were knighted without any ceremony at all.

❖ Squires were often knighted on their way to battle, or even on the battlefield.

❖ In early times, knights or kings would tap squires with their hands. Later, the ceremony was performed using a sword.

Chivalry

The code of behavior that medieval knights were expected to live by was known as chivalry. Knights were expected to be loyal, fight fairly, and act **courteously**.

Knightly Qualities

Knights were supposed to demonstrate many knightly qualities.

❖ *Loyalty and honor.* Knights were expected to keep promises, act in ways that would not bring disgrace upon the family name, and never **betray** their king.

❖ *Christian values.* Knights were Christians who believed that God supported and guided them. They were expected to pray, attend church, and practice Christian values, such as kindness and forgiveness.

❖ *Fairness and courtesy.* Knights were expected to fight fairly. If a knight's opponent fell down, he would give him the opportunity to get up before he continued fighting.

❖ *Good manners.* Knights were expected to be respectful and gracious to women, and courteous at all times.

❖ *Humility.* Knights were not supposed to boast of their achievements and **conquests**.

Squires became knights when a knight or a king dubbed them by tapping them on the shoulder.

WHAT'S IN A NAME?

Chivalry

The word *chivalry* comes from the French word **chevalier**, which means "one who rides a horse."

The Knight's Code of Chivalry

The Knight's Code of Chivalry set out how knights were expected to behave.

The Knight's Code of Chivalry

- ❖ To fear God and maintain His church
- ❖ To serve the king faithfully
- ❖ To protect the weak and defenseless
- ❖ To give assistance to widows and orphans
- ❖ To live by honor and for glory
- ❖ To dislike monetary rewards
- ❖ To fight for the welfare of all
- ❖ To obey those placed in authority
- ❖ To guard the honor of fellow knights
- ❖ To avoid unfairness, meanness, and deceit
- ❖ To speak the truth at all times
- ❖ To persist until the end in any task
- ❖ To respect the honor of women
- ❖ To never refuse a challenge from an equal
- ❖ To never to turn one's back on a foe

Quick Facts

Did Others Know About the Knight's Code of Chivalry?

Others knew about the Knight's Code of Chivalry due to minstrels, poems, and books.

- ❖ Groups of medieval entertainers called minstrels went to castles and sang stories of chivalry. These songs were called Songs of Deeds.
- ❖ During the 1100s, poems called romans became popular. They told tales of knights proving their knightly qualities on quests.
- ❖ By the 1100s, books that described how a knight should behave began to appear.

Minstrels played instruments and sang about chivalrous knights and their achievements.

IN PROFILE: William Marshal

William Marshal came from **humble** beginnings to become the man many describe as 'the greatest knight who ever lived'.

As a young boy, Marshal was apprenticed to the household of William de Tancarville and began his training as a knight. During his career, Marshal's reputation as a chivalrous and **honorable** knight earned him much respect.

Notable Moment

William Marshal served under five kings: Henry II, Henry the Young King, Richard the Lionheart, John III, and Henry III. He was loyal to each of these kings and he won the respect of his **contemporaries** as a result.

What You Should Know About...

William Marshal

❖ When Marshal was young, King Stephen dangled him from a window in order to threaten Marshal's father. The King eventually brought Marshal back inside, and Marshal became known for his bravery during the incident.

❖ Records show that Marshal took part in five hundred jousting tournaments and never lost once.

William Marshal Timeline

1170   1180   1190

1167
Becomes a knight

1187
Promises his loyalty to Henry II and is rewarded with land

Loyalty to King John III

William Marshal is remembered for his loyalty to King John III. After King Richard I died in 1199, William supported John III to become **heir** to the throne. King John III later accused Marshal of being a traitor. He took Marshal's English and Welsh castles and held his two oldest sons as **hostages**. Despite this, Marshal remained loyal to his king. When King John III signed the Magna Carta, Marshal led negotiations for him.

WHAT'S IN A NAME?

Magna Carta

Magna Carta is Latin for "Great Charter" or "Great Paper." This famous document allowed for a king to be challenged if his behavior was seen as **unlawful**. Members of the nobility moved against King John III after deciding that he had been acting unlawfully.

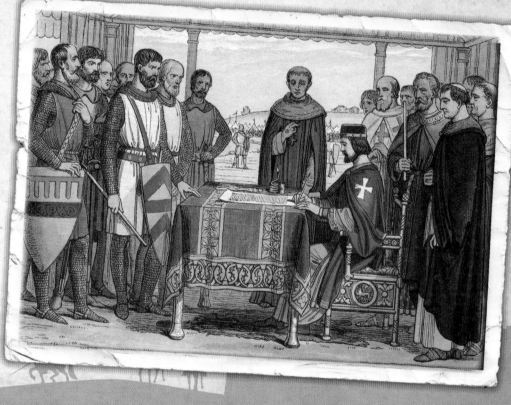

King John III signed the Magna Carta in 1215, following Marshal's negotiations.

1200   1210   1220

1215
Leads **negotiations** to sign the Magna Carta

1216
Chosen **unanimously** to act as **regent** for nine-year-old Henry III after John III's death

1217
Leads his men to victory in the war against Prince Phillip II of France at age seventy. Negotiates the Treaty of Lambeth, which ends the war between England and France.

A Knight's Armor

Knights wore protective armor to increase their chances of survival in battle. Over time, developments in technology and materials changed what knights wore.

Chain Mail

Knights often wore chain mail. Chain mail was a kind of armor made from tiny iron rings that linked together. It protected knights from being pierced with swords. However, it was difficult to care for because the iron would rust quickly. A knight's squire or servants cared for the armor.

Early knights often wore chain mail tunics, known as hauberks. They usually came down over the thighs. Each tunic contained more than 30,000 linked rings and could weigh up to 30 pounds (14 kilograms). A hood, known as a coif, protected the face and neck. During the 1200s, knights began wearing chain mail from head to toe.

Knights wore chain mail beneath their armor to protect their bodies.

Plated Armor

During the 1200s knights began wearing plated armor as protection from lances and arrows. The first plates were made from hardened leather. During the 1300s, leather was replaced with metal. By the 1400s, knights wore suits of plated metal armor for maximum protection. These suits were known as harnesses, and they could weigh up to 55 lbs (25 kg).

Dressing in Plated Armor

A knight dressed in plated armor from the feet upwards. The weight of a suit of armor was easier for a knight to bear as the weight was distributed all over the body.

Besagues were tiny shields that protected the armpits

A breastplate was worn over the chest and a backplate was worn over the back

Vambraces protected the lower arms

Poleyns covered the knee caps

Sabatons protected the feet, and were put on first

Even though his armor was heavy, a knight could still move arond easily when wearing a harness.

The helmet had a skirt of chain mail to protect the neck. Many helmets had visors that could be taken off.

Rerebraces protected the upper arms

Gauntlets had metal plates over the fingers

Cuisses covered the thighs

Greaves protected the calves and ankles

A Knight's Horses and Weapons

Every knight required good horses to ride into battle. Knights also fought with weapons, including spears, lances, and swords.

A Knight's Horses

A knight used his horses for combat, traveling, and competing in jousts and tournaments. A knight's most expensive horse was his warhorse. Warhorses, often known as *destriers*, were usually male stallions that had been trained for combat.

A knight's *destrier* wore armor into battle. Armor for *destriers* was costly but it protected them from lances, swords, and arrows. This armor included:

❖ a shaffron, which covered the horse's head and neck

❖ a high-backed saddle to keep the knight stable

❖ metal plates to protect the horse's chest and rear

❖ trappers or decorative coverings, which often displayed the knight's **coat of arms**

❖ iron horseshoes, which could hurt foot soldiers when the horse reared up

A knight's warhorse wore a shaffron, metal plates, and iron horseshoes into battle.

WHAT'S IN A NAME?

Destrier

The name *destrier* is based on the Latin word *dexter*, which means "right-hand side."

A Knight's Weapons

Knights fought with spears, lances, and swords. A spear was a long pole with a barbed head that often caused more damage when it was removed. A lance was a wooden pole that could pierce a knight's chain mail and knock an opponent off his horse.

Knights fought on foot using swords. Early knights carried a sword in one hand and a shield in the other. These swords were about 31.5 inches (80 centimeters) long. As knights began to wear plated armor, many knights began using heavy swords that were held with two hands, instead of a sword and a shield. These swords were between 59 and 69 in (150 and 175 cm) long.

Early knights used lances and swords to attack opponents, and carried shields for protection.

Quick Facts

What Other Weapons Did Knights Use?
Knights also used maces, wooden stakes, and longbows.

❖ A mace was a spiked metal ball chained to a club. It could deliver blows powerful enough to crush bones when swung at opponents.

❖ Wooden stakes were rammed into the ground. Sometimes horses stepped on these as they charged into battle. The injured horses usually fell, bringing their knights down with them.

❖ Longbows could shoot arrows as far as 984 feet (300 meters). A skilled knight could shoot twelve arrows a minute from a longbow.

Tournaments and Jousts

During times of peace, knights needed to remain fit and keep their skills ready for battle. To do this, knights participated in tournaments and jousts.

Tournaments

Tournaments began as mock, or pretend, battles in which knights could train and demonstrate their battle skills. During these battles, also known as tourneys, two teams of knights would fight one another over a large area of countryside.

The first tournaments began during the 1000s. During these tournaments, knights who won could take their opponents' horses and armor. The losing knight could buy them back. Therefore, knights who were good fighters could make large amounts of money by participating in tournaments. Over time, these battles became popular with ordinary people. By the 1200s they had become a source of entertainment and were considered a sport. The last tournament was held during the 1600s.

Fighting in tournaments helped knights to practice and refine their battle skills.

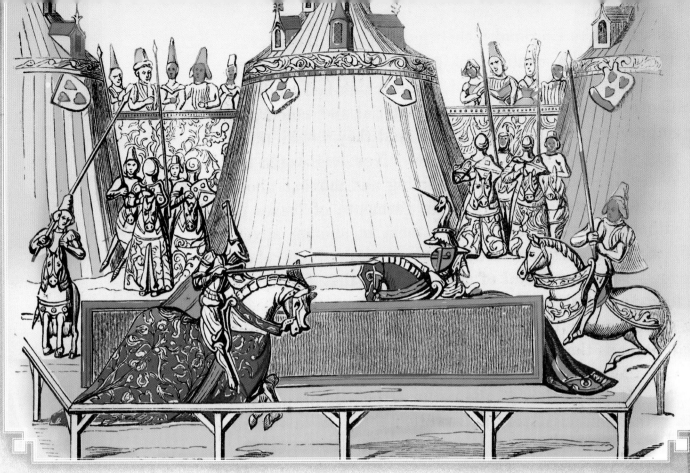

During the 1400s, a barrier called a tilt was used to separate two knights charging toward each other during a joust.

Jousts

Jousts were held from the end of the 1100s until the 1500s. During jousts, two knights fought against each other using lances. The aim was to knock the opponent off his horse. Each knight charged his horse toward his opponent and struck him with a lance. Points could be scored for hitting an opponent's shield and for **dismounting** him. The lances were blunt to protect knights from serious injury or death.

During the 1300s and 1400s, knights sometimes dismounted during jousts and fought in close combat with swords. Participants were only allowed a certain number of blows with their swords. By the 1400s participants also used javelins, maces, and axes.

WHAT'S IN A NAME?

Lists

Jousts were held in areas known as lists. Lists were small, roped-off spaces. Before a joust began, the participants' coats of arms were displayed in the list. If a knight did not play by the rules, his coat of arms was taken down and he could be banned from the list.

SPOTLIGHT ON
the Crusades

Spotlight On

WHAT: The Crusades

ALSO KNOWN AS: The Holy Wars

BEGAN: 1095

ENDED: 1272

The Crusades were a series of religious wars that took place during the Middle Ages. They were fought between Christians and Muslims for control of an area known as the Holy Land in the Middle East. Both sides wanted control of the Holy Land because it contained many important religious sites. Historians believe there were nine major Crusade wars. Knights who fought in these wars were known as crusader knights.

Crusader knights were Christian knights who fought during the Crusades.

The Beginning of the Crusades

In 1040, the Holy Land was conquered by Muslim leaders. These leaders forced Christians to leave the Holy Land. Across Europe, Christian leaders began to fear that the Muslim leaders would try to take over parts of Europe as well. On November 27, 1095, Pope Urban II launched the first Crusade. He planned to defeat the Muslim leaders in Syria and Palestine and eventually claim Jerusalem.

The Crusades Timeline

1050	1100	1150

1096–1099
The first Crusade, launched by Pope Urban II

1147–1149
The second Crusade, launched by King Louis VII of England and Conrad III of Germany

1189–1192
The third Crusade, launched by Pope Gregory VIII. It was led by King Richard I of England, King Phillip II of France, and Holy Roman Emperor Frederick I.

The Outcome of the Crusades

Crusader knights never gained control of the Holy Land, despite years of battle. During the first war, crusaders defeated the Muslims and claimed many cities. However, the Muslims began to fight back and, in 1144, they reclaimed a **county** called Edessa. During the second war, the Muslims reclaimed much of the territory they had lost, including Jerusalem. A further seven wars were fought but the knights failed to regain control of Jerusalem.

What You Should Know About...

The Crusades

❖ The most famous Muslim leader was Salah al Din Yusuf ibn Ayyub, also known as Saladin. During the second Crusade war, he took control of Jerusalem but did not harm any Christians.

❖ During the third war, King Richard I negotiated a peace settlement that allowed Christian **pilgrims** to enter the Holy Land.

❖ In this same war, King Richard I and his men were left to fight alone. Emperor Frederick I died while bathing in a creek and his soldiers returned home. King Phillip I and his men returned to France.

This painting shows crusader knights entering the county of Edessa (in modern-day Turkey) after they captured it in 1098.

1218–1221
The fifth Crusade, planned by the fourth council of the Lateran

1248–1254
The seventh Crusade, launched by King Louis IX of France

1271–72
The ninth Crusade, launched by King Edward of England

1200   1250   1300

1201–1204
The fourth Crusade, launched by Pope Innocent III

1228–1229
The sixth Crusade, launched by Emperor Frederick II

1270
The eighth Crusade, launched by King Louis IX of France

Religious Knights

During the Crusades, groups of crusader knights were formed. These knights **pledged** themselves to God and their armor was decorated with the Christian cross. There were three main groups of crusader knights: the Knights Hospitaller, the Teutonic Knights, and the Knights Templar.

The Knights Hospitaller

In 1080, the Knights Hospitaller, or the Knights of St. John, was established to care for sick and poor pilgrims in the Holy Land. Soon after, they began to **escort** these pilgrims on their travels through the Holy Land. During the first Crusade they became a military religious order. The Knights Hospitaller fought to defend the Holy Land, and they wore black coats with a white cross into battle.

The Teutonic Knights

At the end of the 1100s, a German religious order known as the Teutonic Knights was formed. The order was originally established to care for sick pilgrims in a German hospital in the Holy Land. However, they soon began to fight throughout eastern Europe, claiming territory and **converting** people to Christianity.

Religious knights, such as the Templar knight shown here, could be recognized by the Christian crosses on their coats and tunics.

The Knights Templar

During the 1100s, a military religious order called the Knights Templar was established. These knights lived in the Al-Aqsa Mosque on Temple Mount in Jerusalem. They turned the mosque, which was a Muslim place of worship, into a Christian church and named it the Temple of the Lord.

The Knights Templar were **elite** warriors who fought in many key battles during the Crusades. They would charge on horseback to break down **enemy lines**. Their beliefs forbade them from retreating in battle. The Knights Templar's most notable victory occurred at the Battle of Montgisard in 1177, when approximately 500 knights helped to defeat an army of more than 26,000 soldiers.

Quick Facts

Were the Knights Templar Wealthy?

The Knights Templar became very wealthy, and this wealth led to the order being **disbanded**.

❖ The knights created the first banking system, offering people loans and charging **interest**. Eventually, they became so wealthy they attracted negative attention from some kings and nobles.

❖ In the early 1300s, King Phillip IV of France accused the Knights Templar of worshipping the devil. They were forced to disband and some were even burned at the stake.

Templar knights became some of the most powerful and wealthy Christians in the Holy Land.

IN PROFILE: King Richard I

— In Profile —

WHAT: King Richard I
ALSO KNOWN AS: Richard the Lionheart
BEGAN: 1157
ENDED: 1199

King Richard I is remembered as one of England's great warrior kings. He reigned from 1189 to 1199, yet during these years he spent no longer than six months in England. For most of his reign, King Richard I was fighting in battles during the Crusades.

King Richard I is remembered for attacking the city of Acre in the Holy Land and for defeating the Muslim leader known as Saladin. For many years after this battle, King Richard I remained in the Holy Land fighting battles and defending the territory he had won. His bravery and courage earned him the nickname Richard the Lionheart.

Notable Moment

In 1192, King Richard I negotiated a three-year truce with Saladin. The treaty allowed Christian pilgrims to enter Jerusalem once again.

King Richard I Timeline

1185

1188

1191

1187
Begins fighting in the Crusades

1191
Attacks the city of Acre, defeats Saladin's army at the Battle of Arsuf, and negotiates a peace treaty with Saladin

A King Imprisoned

After fighting in the third Crusade war, King Richard I began his journey home to England. Rough seas took his ship off course and he was washed ashore in Austria. There, he was captured and imprisoned in Duke Leopold's castle. The Emperor of Germany paid the large sum of 75,000 marks to secure King Richard I's release and took him to Germany. The English then paid a **ransom** of 150,000 marks to return King Richard I to England. This large amount of money was around one-fifth of England's total wealth, and it put a strain on the country's economy.

What You Should Know About...

King Richard I

❖ The first battle that King Richard I fought was against his father. He formed an **alliance** with his brothers and they attacked their father. The attack failed and Richard was stripped of his title of duke.

❖ It is said that on his deathbed King Richard I **pardoned** the archer who fatally shot him with an arrow.

1194	1197	1200

1192
Imprisoned by Duke Leopold and sold to Germany

1194
Returns to England after a ransom is paid to Germany

1199
Dies after being shot by an archer

Heraldry

When a knight was dressed in full armor, it was hard to recognize him on the battlefield. Therefore, each knight began using a coat of arms as his symbol. This system of identification was known as heraldry.

Coat of Arms

Each coat of arms belonged to a different family and could not be passed to an outsider. Upon a knight's death, his coat of arms passed to his eldest son. Younger brothers would usually modify the family coat of arms by adding a symbol to represent themselves. When a noblewoman married a knight, her coat of arms was often added to the right side of her husband's shield.

A knight's coat of arms was originally placed on his armor so that others could recognize him on the battlefield. Then coats of arms were placed on shields, weapons, and armor, and on cloth tunics that were draped over warhorses. They were also used as a stamp for official documents.

The medieval knight Simon de Montford had a roaring lion on his coat of arms.

Elements of the Coat of Arms

Each coat of arms had a unique design. However, all coats of arms had the same basic elements.

❖ The background color was known as the field. Originally only green, red, blue, black, gold, and silver could be used for the field. Over time, patterned backgrounds that mixed several colors began to emerge.

❖ The bands of color that appeared on the field were known as ordinaries. They could be different shapes.

❖ The picture in the center of the shield was called the charge. It was usually an animal or a pattern.

A traditional coat of arms was made up of a field, ordinaries, and a charge.

SPOTLIGHT ON
Famous Battles

Many battles were fought during the Middle Ages. The most significant battles include the Battle of Hastings, the Siege of Jerusalem, the Battle of Agincourt, and the Battle of Bosworth.

The Battle of Hastings

The Battle of Hastings is considered the most **decisive** battle in the conquest of England. It took place between the English and the Normans in 1066. The English side, led by King Harold II, had approximately 5,000 soldiers who were still weary from fighting in an earlier battle. They formed a wall with their shields and took blow after blow as 15,000 Norman soldiers attempted to break through. Eventually, the Normans did break through and defeated them.

The Siege of Jerusalem

The Siege of Jerusalem was the most important victory for the crusaders during the first Crusade war. It took place between the crusaders and the Muslims in 1099. More than 100,000 crusaders took control of the city of Jerusalem and held it against enemy attack for five weeks. The Siege of Jerusalem was one of few victories for the crusaders during the Crusades.

It is believed that King Harold II was killed by an arrow shot into his eye during the Battle of Hastings.

The English won the Battle of Agincourt despite having fewer soldiers than the French army they were fighting against.

The Battle of Agincourt

The Battle of Agincourt was one of the bloodiest battles of the Hundred Years' War. It took place between England and France in 1415. King Henry V and his men arrived in France and, on the way to Agincourt, they took control of the town of Harfeur. By the time the English arrived at Agincourt, their numbers were significantly **depleted**. Some records suggest that they only had 5,000 knights when they launched into battle against more than 30,000 French knights. However, the French were defeated during a swift and bloody battle.

The Battle of Bosworth

The Battle of Bosworth ended the War of the Roses, a thirty-year war between two branches of the same family. It took place between the House of Lancaster and the House of York in 1485. During this battle, Henry Tudor, who was from the House of Lancaster, defeated King Richard I, who was from the House of York. King Richard I was killed and he became the last English king to die in battle. Henry Tudor became king after his death.

The Decline of the Medieval Knights

By the 1500s many countries had begun developing large armies of professional soldiers. Professional soldiers fought differently than knights, and filled a paid position, rather than one of nobility. Over time, these soldiers began to replace medieval knights. Eventually the title of knight became a social position.

The Rise of Professional Soldiers

During the 1500s, changes in battle tactics, weapons, and armor gave rise to professional soldiers. These soldiers fought mostly on foot, did not wear suits of armor, and used different weapons, including firearms.

The Social Position of Knights

Over time, the role of the knight became associated with honor. It was granted to people that the reigning king or queen felt should be recognized for their achievements. Today, the title of knight is no longer handed down through families and does not only belong to those in the nobility. Instead, knighthoods are awarded to people who have made outstanding contributions to society. People who have received knighthoods in recent times include:

❖ former secretary of state Colin Powell
❖ director Steven Spielberg
❖ singer Sir Paul McCartney
❖ computer mogul Bill Gates

Over time, there was less demand for knights to fight in large battles such as this.

Glossary

alliance   An agreement between two or more people.

allies   People or groups that support another person or group in battle.

apprenticeship   A period during which a boy learns how to become a knight.

betray   Be disloyal or dishonest to another.

coat of arms   Emblems that were used to identify knights.

conquests   Territory or land that has been taken by force.

consolidated   United into one system.

contemporaries   People who live during the same period of time.

converting   Convincing or persuading people to adopt other beliefs.

county   A large area of land.

courteously   Politely and considerately.

decisive   Having power to change the course of events.

depleted   Reduced.

disbanded   Split up and separated.

dismounting   Getting off a horse.

elite   The best or most skilled.

enemy lines   The front lines of soldiers in an enemy's army.

escort   Guide and protect another.

heir   A person who inherits wealth or a title from their family.

honorable   Worthy of respect.

hostage   A person who is taken prisoner in order to bargain with the other side.

humble   Low in social standing.

interest   A fee charged on money that has been loaned.

jousting   A competition in which two mounted knights armed with lances charge at each other.

lance   A long pole with a sharp end, used for stabbing opponents.

military campaigns   Series of military operations to achieve a particular goal.

mounted   On horseback.

negotiations   Discussions between groups to decide on an outcome.

nobility   People with certain titles, such as knights, lords, and ladies.

pardoned   Gave official forgiveness as the king.

pilgrims   People who journey to visit a sacred or holy place.

pledged   Swearing a solemn promise or oath to do something.

ransom   Money demanded to return a person who is being held prisoner.

regent   A person who serves as king in the absence of the real king.

reign   The period during which a king or queen rules.

religious order   A community of Christian people who live together and are recognized by the Church as an order.

Saxons   People from northern Germany who invaded England in the 500s and 600s.

territory   A large area of land.

tournaments   A series of contests in which people compete against one another until there is one winner.

unanimously   All people or groups in agreement.

unlawful   Illegal or against the law.

warriors   Expert fighters in battle.

Index